Brownsville

Brownsville

Poems by
Martin Itzkowitz

Printed in the United States.

Cover and book design by Asya Blue Design.

Cover photo courtesy Municipal Archives, City of New York

ISBN 979-8-9901881-7-4 Hardcover Casebound
ISBN 979-8-9901881-8-1 Paperback
ISBN 979-8-9901881-9-8 Ebook

To the friends of my youth . . .
and to the memories of those now gone

Contents

cabbage 1
autograph 1: spaces 2
Reelpolitik 3
borderlands 1 4
territorial imperative. 6
Russians 7
autograph 2 9
homage to mrs plochman. 10
playground. 11
festival jazz 12
Manifest Destiny 13
Peddlers 14
autograph 3 16
hymnoid for hyman g. 17
borderlands 2: the avenue/winter night 18
whet whether 21
epitaphs for the early dead 22
powerhouse 25
Menakhem Mendel 26
autograph 4: reading room 28
trumpeter. 29
lunar litany. 30

The Ballad of Harry Heller. 31
Vendor: Venit, Vincit 34
upon exchange 35
autograph 5: from The Book of Canines Chapter XI 36
field of dreams 38
auntiquities 39
damaged goods. 41
autograph 6: childsplay 42
the greatest show on earth 43
diamond. 46
sabbath service 48
clean-press, jerk 50
Italians 51
autograph 7: kiss 1 54
suicides. 55
enterprise 57
the-ater. 57
lullaby 58
jailbird jack 59
autograph 8: transformation. 60
barbershop 61
borderlands 3 62
witness 63
autograph 9: triple play 65
Buck Weinstein 66
autograph 10: nocturne 69
delis 70
Recollection 72
Glossary and Notes 73
Acknowledgments 77

Prefatory Note

Brownsville is a neighborhood in Brooklyn. Its population in the era to which these poems refer, were, for the most part, immigrants from southern and eastern Europe, overwhelmingly Jewish, and two generations of their descendants.

cabbage

at 5:15 at *515*
whiff of cooking cabbage
drifts through dimlit halls
clings to clothes and skin
seeps through porous walls
and leaving pallid pátinas
of sickly green
all sense appalls

pottage of poverty
(with roots and tubers
livers and lights)
essences of earth
and life transported
new world/known dearth
if salt-and-peppered
otherwise unspiced

what hope—at last recourse—
that from some leavened loaf
a sugared scent might rise
cinnamon—apples—
in sprinkled seasons
and for moments small and scant
our cabbage lives disguise

———

autograph 1: spaces

no vacancies in empty lots
while weeds fulfill
a breathless festering
profuse upon a graveled patch
where cluckless peckstrut hens
scratch insensible
to padded passages
of vagrant cats

deadhush
winds of evening baffled by brush
ailanthus loom unwavering
athwart the moon
as mist moves mystical
through window screens

fast in shadowed caverns
of ancient memory
clouded—colorless—
a child conceives the grass

———

Reelpolitik

One eye bulged and Sidney Greenstreet fat,
Old Kaplan lurked upon his checkered stoop,
All Charlie-Channed beneath a pale straw hat.

Lorre-like, his voice a shy-tongued catch,
He lured each raucous idler, whispering "shpilst?"
And subtly made but never met his match.

Magnanimous as Bogart with a gun,
He graciously accepted red or black,
But crowed in secret Cagney game begun,

Where bat-swift passing to Lugosi grin,
He swept the board with counselled king on king
 And jugularly struck at last to win.

For penalty, his victim put to pains,
Went fatefully to fetch the Freiheit in,
Karlovian, aclank in mental chains.

Thumbing through the smallprint of his days,
Old Kaplan read the politics of power
Between abstracted lines of gabby haze.

———

borderlands 1

Southerly—past trolley carbarn terminals
The Boulevard—endless as adolescence
Scruffed median in growth of patchy green
Rolls on in routed ritual toward secret Queens
As disenchanted in the gasp of August evenings
Awaiting her awhirr on Werther wings
He goes past Hinsdale Street and hope
Though savoring his summerslove in dusky dreams

"Mister, can you cross me?" Passage rights
Initiate to misteries at seventeen

Then plodfoot on till four gas stations meet
And Pennsylvania slopes pitfallen toward the sea
Asphalt sucked down summerstenching creeks
While everysided marshgrassfields in wanbloom
Bow to pallid breezes, feinting light
Till cut autumnally for Succoth huts—
Scrapwood walls with thatch of sheerest sheaves

But sooner, through furnaces of Danieled days
The child transported—bare back to hairshirt seat—
At open window of his uncle's Chevrolet
Borne by Boulevard and sunken street
To earthsedge splintered at Canarsie pier
Where on folding chairs grandparents sat in state
Silent—turned toward Europe and old home:

Below, the sea in monotone rolled gray on gray
Though for cataract of mind or years
No living eye could see past Rockaway.

——————

territorial imperative

land war confined
to metes and bounds
of pen-knived lines
attack and plunder:
steelsedge wellaimed
wedged in foreign soil—
dominioned enemy
soon carved asunder
though desperate sweep
of rival's heel
might cancel all

but wonder:
which estate
(materiel or mind)
was real
and which a blunder

Russians

In a low-slung house
Narrowly detached
Preserved their peasantry.

Their old man, eyes opaque and iris white,
Would sit for hours in his weedy lot
L-bent from the backyard to the street,
Guarding hens from alley cats and boys,
Worn cane laid rifle-like across his knee,
Or later, losing half a cankered leg,
A makeshift crutch—with black stump pipe
At steady puff between determined jaws.

The woman, more malevolent in view,
Babushkaed, or with steely hair pulled back,
As if to fully bare her bulbous nose—
Brown mole studded where one nostril flared—
Would, angered at the gazing of a child
Whose wonder rose to overwhelm his fear,
Grunt hoarse curses, bulge her sow-eyed glare,
Though the fleshed-out baseball at her throat
Fascinated more for trembling there.

Her daughter, it was said, in World War 2
Turned open antisemite in the streets,
Lamenting so much Christian blood was shed
To save the worthless, troublemaking Jews.

If after Goldman's son was killed, and Hahn's,
And Lerner's twins, she stopped her noise,
Their weight still failed to straighten out her
Hakenkreuz.

———

autograph 2

heshy hit me
Hit him back

he ran away
Catch him then

he runs too fast
Wait till he stops

first the balloon was red
then it got smaller and blue
then yellowy pink like before

heshy don't hear good no more
maybe now he'll listen

———

homage to mrs plochman

in processional
of weekdaywheelscreak
or steelcaphoofrim's clap
resonant for holyhush
of friday fouroclocks
she bore behind
with spatula and pan
timescour sanctified
to mark twistyeasting
horseloaves free from stain
of sparrowswoop or strike
and scoop as hers
by covenanted rite
to fruit and multiply
for slowsand seasons down
her canaancorner yard
before newquickened kindling
of sabbath lights
that no fall leaf should wither
nor springfired bush consume

———

playground

saturday rammy
for nanny goat park
steelstunt pastoral
bare cityscape of
sand swing slide
figured in concrete ground
where monkeybarred and
calibanned agrope
descent suspended
incomplete we ape
the witless girl be
low inclined in chor
us each by each ass
ents to evil aye

———

festival jazz

the villagers of Ostrolenk
a congregation come
four thousand miles
in wholesale haul
remembered ritely
how to hold a bash

brass spitoons spit polished
and railings of the central stage
festooned with parti-colored lights:
themselves all spiffed
with hats full-plumed or blooming
glad-ragged in decorous delight
yet all atwitch atwitter,
toes expectantly atap
as if in decorum's spite

until—at last—their headman,
ninety if a day—horn-handed—
bearded, shawled, and capped,
stepped up, raised his axe, and blew:
te-ki-ah sheh-vah-rim te-ru-ah--
four-thousand-year-old riff
of a new year blast

Manifest Destiny

Grandfather's first forefinger joint
Bent at near right angle to the rest—
Pointless—an anvil accident—
No maimed attempt to free himself
From service in the army of the czar.
Grandmother lost a little finger
(Blood poisoning set in)
To an iffy kitchen knife and sanitary scalpel—
Left a knob
Between twin whiffs of ether and carbolic swab.
Sammy G. gave up a knuckle to a Nazi bullet
(Dicey business—war—)
While at his workbench cousin Jack was reft
Of several more—
Betrayed by reckless inattention
And a fickle saw.
Vicissitudes too great
To clench a common fist
Against a common fate.

———

Peddlers

(i)

Struhberris—fresh—struhberris!
Yeh, I'm waitin' lady—don' rosh.
You got deh moneh, honeh,
I got deh time.

(ii)

It was the horse—belgian—clydesdale
somewhere in its veins
worthy to be shod of felix randal

its member thickly long descending
and we bent stiflehigh
standing in prepubescent awe
of surgent stream in gallonspour

though (then unknown)
undone to docile dray
a hulk in haul of harness handle.

(iii)

Bananos!—ripe bananos—heah!
a singlesong of solo crop
for aftermath of war
quick march behind past fear
unarmored open cart
with store of shells
noplosive yellowing
toward brownsoft sheer
down infantry of streets
mindswept paths all clear

Bananos!—ripe bananos—heah!

———

autograph 3

before the blond radio
black head bowed
roosevelt dead in georgia
her own warm springs

———

hymnoid for hyman g

passing the pale and palestine
he stood at last transfixed in his travail

literate in four tongues
he sliced salami

swift at calculation
he schemed against mice

confined to narrow scale and scope
he gauged all weight with measured sight

bound by rule of shelf and row
he set small store by philosophy

lament in monotone
all possibilities betrayed in one:
ashen elegies of gray
sackcloth psalms of dun

———

borderlands 2: the avenue/winter night

"say hey, piet, what boogie-woogie now?"

street of light
incandescent—neon—flood
shop windows white
red—blue—green above
glow—pulse—flash
all mannered
awhirl in razzle
on loew's marquee
sequences aswirl
in fullest dazzle

yellow streetlamps mellow
but cars and buses
bug-eyed glare
with cyclops trolleys
in their single stare/
cigarette—cigar ends
dot the dark
and oven glow
from coal-grate mouths
of sweet potato carts
as off odd corners
steel drum sconces
blaze against the cold

before the savings bank
huddlers themselves inflamed
with talk of war and whether
strikes—lynchings—rights
whatever in the news
affirms—denies—sanctifies—profanes
their several anathemas—creeds—views
gather and remain/
others pass—some striding
brilliant in their dress
fete—at restaurant
or wedding hall—assured:
sequins shimmer—
feathers in fedoras iridesce/
more move in staccato—
step and halt—
for luster of a pair of patent shoes—
fur—hat—a sabbath suit

at edges of the scene—
less resolute—
others hope for halo
in suffusion of a scattered beam/
a few—pillars perhaps
on which the world depends—
seek with steady gait and inner eye
some rarer fire that transcends

these—by whichever light—
shoppers, window and real—
corner talkers—passersby—
sole strollers—youthful clusters—pairs—
hawkers—merchants—moviegoers—
wedding guests—and diners—
each and all illumined
full willed and blent
(despite a thousand disparate strivings)
in quest for stuff and spirit
of survival and ascent—
destinies envisioned or past sight—
these—oh papa walt—
flare—flicker—or flame—
these are your flambeaus of the night

———————

whet whether

double wheel backborne
and counterground
september's sunwane
tishri's moonrise year
he went his round
of succothscythe and time's
edging abram's knife
or sarah's shear
ringing brassbelled chimes
for isaacsblood
no ramshorn near

———————

epitaphs for the early dead

(for c. k.)

when word spread
that he was dead
tossed by a tailgate's chance—
flung by his own exuberant excess
all stood shrouded
in self-cast pall
impressed by their recall
of great laughter
muscle, hands, jaw
and (most) of gentleness

(for j. l.)

we never knew for sure
if a baseball struck his head
or bullets of another sort
unseen within
swelled the brain
and stiffened him
until he had no breath

but on the day of death
his friends hovered
at the candy store
(no place of succor then)
comfortless in crowd
and at each passerby

would shriek in hawking cry
"going to j's funeral?"
and as if plying grief
for no demur at all
would be denied

long afterward
his mother went in silence
and with empty eye

(for n. t.)

those who sat behind her
staring at the motion
of the stripes she wore
(a mazing black and white)
saw as she herself did
more and more—bedazzled—
vacantly— as if through haze—
while in sickly sympathy
a deafened ear a thickened tongue
misheard misspoke in stutter
to derision of the rowdy boys
their laughter—like all words—
misperceived as utterance
of merest noise

beside her bed stood six
aware of death

(as receded to shred edges
of a remnant brain
in slumber lying
she was not)

but wakened now
to dying

(for ?)

whose brother was it
crushed under
a dump truck
blood forever
darkening our grieving streets?

———

powerhouse

heart of the dynamoed dark
brassfireglinting past
forbidden gratemesh gates
as shadow priests in sacrifice
of sinew, spirit, sweat
to mosthighwinding turbines
bow bare backs, bare heads

beyond unaltared rails
black masses still unspoken
herd in tenemental prayer
timbrelled track on wheel
sole hallelu for soul's hosanna
while eyes yet unannealed
openwindowed doubleportioned
grope in lour or leer—sourceward
as israelites their sixth day sabbath manna

———

Menakhem Mendel

Menachem Mendel, one house from the corner,
Lived at the edge of eccentricity;
The sort of fellow, slit-eyes weakly blue,
Who after shaving seemed to need a shave
And stirred suspicion by his looks alone.
His dress was ill arranged—winter and summer—
The same white shirt, blue suit and tie—rumpled,
Wrinkled, and awry—with just his gray hat changed
From felt to straw, although still worn atilt
With brim bent asymmetrically aside.

But maybe not as sloven as he seemed,
Since sidewalk sitters on a summer night
Could hear him shout to Rokhel for his soaps—
Three separate bars for hands and feet and face;
"Where's the soap for your tokhes?" one would call
To laughter and the rattle of a shade.

Wasn't any doubt his car was clean—
A forty-eight De Soto brightly blue;
Whitewalls spotless too; though when he washed it
Wasn't clear. Still, most had seen him drive,
Morning and evening twice around the block,
Rolling up three hundred miles a year.

His Sabbath route was also long enough,
A catty-cornered walk across the street
For mumbled prayer and pious pinch of snuff.

———

autograph 4: reading room

silent on Stone
old oakwood shelves
forbidwhisper
fearful of elves

still mindmurmurs
soulsweeps windrush will
as boyswift he horsehearted
king of the wind
stallioned black or roan
in blurlight stands
eyestrained down greenshade
mistyng for Chincoteague

trumpeter

chillblast
dentbelled brassnotes
burst icelipped
in stiffwind spurts
down january's alley
bounded volley sounded
back along rime walls
while cats in scatter
crash no cymbal sympathy
in scurried snowruff irony
of trashcan clatter

notes penetrant as flake or chip
pass valves of rattleglass
and rise to ring past radiator's hiss
and fail to sing—yet chafe
a heartsearshand in zeroing
to range accord in chainsash strain
and clinking sparechange fling

an interval of trumpetuck
as smallcoin tremble through
fumblegrovel fingers
of unglovely blue
and scuffshuffle feet
recede in smart progression
proceed in sharp retreat

lunar litany

scarcely seen through narrow passages
between spent slabs of tenements
above all lamplit sheen of tardark streets
new moon—queen of time and tides—
draws ancient men from synagogues to sing
on sidewalks under clothesline skies

their thrust and sway in zionprayer belie
atonement of all antique sacrifice
and wailing cries betray a primal call
for ishtar's arms as paradise

rounds of time in seablood's surge
renew the manner of men's prime
and supple thews of memory
past antiquity of jews to eldest urge

———

The Ballad of Harry Heller

Born beyond the tenements,
But still of low degree,
He gave no signal early on
Of prowess yet to be.

> *When standing tall he tossed the ball*
> *Then struck it hard and clean,*
> *And Harry Heller hit two sewers*
> *With a hi-bounce pink spaldeen.*

Restless, raucous, driven child
Of both his time and place,
He joined aflit from street to street
In childhood's earnest chase.

> *Till standing tall he tossed the ball*
> *Then struck it hard and clean,*
> *And Harry Heller hit two sewers*
> *With a hi-bounce pink spaldeen.*

Diligent enough at school
(No scholar, sage, or seer)
He thought to be a pharmacist?
Accountant? (choice unclear).

Though standing tall he tossed the ball
Then struck it hard and clean,
And Harry Heller hit two sewers
With a hi-bounce pink spaldeen.

Success in moderation came,
A spouse and children too.
Though status and address had changed,
He was that stalwart who

Once standing tall had tossed the ball
Then struck it hard and clean,
And Harry Heller hit two sewers
With a hi-bounce pink spaldeen.

At ease in his retirement
To mountainside or sea,
He often smiled as he recalled
And sipped a glass of tea

How standing tall he tossed the ball
Then struck it hard and clean,
And Harry Heller hit two sewers
With a hi-bounce pink spaldeen.

Three score years and ten or more
And he is past and gone.
In minds of those who witnessed it
His triumph still lives on.

> *For standing tall he tossed the ball*
> *Then struck it hard and clean,*
> *And Harry Heller hit two sewers*
> *With a hi-bounce pink spaldeen.*

When witnesses themselves decline
And all their days are done,
Who then will hold the memory?
A nullifying none.

> *Who's this Harry Heller guy?*
> And what does "two sewers" mean?
> Why should someone give a damn?
> And what's a "pink spaldeen"?

———

Vendor: Venit, Vincit

Leather-dark against a uniform
stark white—gold tooth resplendent in full sun
or flashed in flicker of a lamplit evening,
he brought to panting summer days
cold comfort: root beer popsicles,
sundaes (pick a flavor) in a cup,
thick wedges of tortoni—and always
a token to be saved, collected, then redeemed
(a dozen days or so) as free confection—
with signs of further favor every time:
crepe paper fans in arcing rainbow,
Jacob's ladders, Chinese finger traps,
tattoos—worn, washed away, renewed
(however pale) in second transfer.
To him small profit (so we thought)
for our far greater gain.
In other iconography or faith
he should have been Archangel Andy—or
of ice-cream our Sicilian patron saint.

——

upon exchange

pit dug shallowly
to hold all marbles cast
(filberts seasonally)
in head-to-head or knee-to-knee
conveyance of commodity
numbers tallied and surpassed

lost—all lost—
in vacant lots no hedge
against hegemony

———

autograph 5:
from The Book of Canines Chapter XI

[9]And Snooky the Pomeranian, known among all elders as a wanderer of streets, begat many dogs and bitches throughout the land. [10]Upon Shadow, the spaniel-poodle, he begat a litter, among them Teddy, who sang mightily to music on the radio, and Spot, who would return a hundred miles in search of ancient masters. [11]But last and chiefly there was Duke, fair and silken- haired in the image of his sire, who remained in his household of birth after Shadow, his dam, was struck by a car and with scant ceremony placed in an ash can, black hair limp in the breeze like flags of mourning. [12]And Duke after three years golden shared her fate, but lingered three days to die in the week his master's second son was born. [13]Then Myron, his master, and Myron's nephew, Arnold the unwashed, bore Duke down to bury him in a lot beside the carbarns. [14]And the child, Myron's first born, wept for Duke thirty days. Yea, even unto sixty days he mourned. [15]Thereafter, his brother's birth and Duke's death were as one in the child's mind. [16]Still, he would search the bin beneath the kitchen window to stroke the leash now useless beside the stored potatoes. [17]Then in all the tenement just one dog more survived, Boopsie, Eskimo Spitz of Red Rosen and his mother, she who of old at work at the A&P had defied the rules of rationing. [18]And it came to pass that Snooky, full of years, left on a last journey, far-wandering, never to return. [19]But past due days of grieving, came another in his stead to the house of that old prizefighter, Herman

Held, a brindle boxer, Pugsy, aptly named. [20]Now Duke's sire and dam were dead and he deceased without issue, yet his kindred survived in the land. [21]Among the chief of these was Pancho, the lamb-coated, in a household new removed from Tennessee, the mother, marked by Harry Truman glasses and a drawl, with her two sons, Pauley and Jerome. [22]And as he walked, Jerome's hips rolled as a ship at sea, provoking whispers and smirks among the people. [23]There were as well, Cisco and Sugar, fox terriers paired in pedigree and led on double leash by Mrs. Więcek, who in children's dreams proffered them her broom and bade them fly away. [24]Then secretly, learnéd in the lore of TV westerns, the child pondered how Sugar had drawn Cisco from Pancho; though he said nothing, and the mystery endured. [25]But among the least of kindred there was Prince, misnamed, lop-eared, scrawn in the family Lack, while at the ground floor window past the grocery, dwelt a cur without name, a great harasser of passersby, as his mistress was of tenants. [26]Yet, at intervals after the passing of Duke, sounds of howling rang across the silences of empty lots. [27]Some said it was the child bereft calling to his lost dog beyond the heavens; and some said it was the voice of lamentation filling all vastnesses of vacancy.

field of dreams

rusted junker
single wheeled (within)
hubless hunkers

boys' refuge afternoons
whilemothershop
steered submarine and plunge
or rocketshot past moon
unmoving—disengauged—ungeared

or arear
youngmates' nighthaven
in their coupling
throttle (seemingly) athrob
thrusting (as if) toward destiny
of heaven paradise or eden
till surcease

unengined still (none engendered)
unfueled despite all spill
at rest confined (en fin)
to sagseats of erstwhile clunker
condom and car
used random strewn
abandoned sans civility
lie scattered graves
of phantom possibility

auntiquities

some could not forgive
the brown floor soap
used to wash her face
the dentures laid
beside her dinner plate
the litany of "ain't"
her utter domesticity
and lower east side taint

some could not forget
her visits once a month
complete with gifts
of dime store candy
coloring books and crayons
for the kids
talk of this and that
a horsey laugh
above the sound of dishes
washed unasked

some unsettled still
in new prosperities
of mind and means
could not risk (they felt)
a backward glance—
fearful of salt
and shattered mirrors—
so, once uncle o was gone

and she fallen, failed
in suicide attempt
they left her
ward of wards
long decades
after all repair was done

some on certain sundays
rode long slow rails
toward kings park
bearing small news—themselves—
and corned beef sandwiches

———————

damaged goods

staincapped
stubblefaced
lacktooth
shy of bone

he pushed
his battered pram
onewheel
elliptical

pausing at odd
intervals
for passing patrons
random—quondam

pulling (then)
from cartoned cargo
(cardboard crushed)
seconds of socks

———

autograph 6: childsplay

hands
brown
white
tan
over
hands
clasp
steel
sticks
last
to
grasp
spin
three
times
over
head
win

subwaycars

———

the greatest show on earth

down saddened streets of spring—
gray and barelygreen for shoots
of paleweed shuddering
through cracks in walks and walls
or timidly in tuft atop
a gravel mound or piled debris—
as if to muffled drums
beyond a wagonsrock
or rough rust rhythm
of enjangled bells
the sorrowful circus comes

. . .

a painted pony leads
in lame excuse for such publicity
his master's lens accrues
among the sparse and curblined crowd
of scattered twos and threes
though child on child astride in his epiphany
utters with his eyes a palomino prayer
or smirks in scrubhorse villainy
and none aware of scrawls behind
hard-spelled upon the barricades
of dunbrick walls

. . .

a pair of spotted dogs
wheel a wicker pram
in squeals of pain
and dropping to all fours
accept a biscuit bone
to scant applause
then in repertoire by rote
of playjump rollfrog
leaphoop overdead
close with hindlegged waltz
in formal dress of ragged bows

their tamer doffs his cap
a few toss in a cent or two
while others glumly
weigh performance done
against expectant licorice whip
or stick of gum

troupe moving on with gathered gear
still plays someothercornerwhere
still under canvas gaze

. . .

aprowl upon the night
menageries are loose
down alleys of the dark
aware of whiskerspace

for lack of light
till glinting eye on eye
should spark ignite
in seasonshreik of lust
to pounce for necknervesnumb
and mounting thrust

then dangering by day
for stoop or clattercan
in low swagbellied sway
till secret littering of seed
is spread in full fecundity
down each childscuttered street

. . .

and we in sideshow peep
through stunted destiny
or stand immovably obese
agape to swallow
sword or fire dreams
though scars of each on each
tattoo our souls indelibly

————

diamond

behind scarred trolley barns
among weeds upon sparesand
over bones of buried dogs
baseball boys renew each spring
loose uniform of poloshirt
perchance odd jeans
abloom in capped caprice
all cleatlesskedded as if clogged

afield glovethwack
chatter above bent knees
they catch at threads
—rizzuto—reiser—reese
of modern mysteries

at bat a taunt: no hit no hit
but dauntless swinging taut
as avatars of mantraed power
 —mantle—mays—mize
though best abed (twinite)
in silent colloquy
with ancient of days just past—
joe d.

at last hardbrake
whips wire from reel
(alas) rips wheel from track
swiftstopped wristwrench

batscrackwebsrift—rend
(what gear or tack unscathed)
smallmound groundswell
heaves in wind or rain
as if in quake
spilling grave debris
emblem oblique: finality—
summersend dreamerswake

———

sabbath service

odors of candlewax—
sweet-wine—snuff
hover above half numbing
chant chatter and hum
of two half-alien tongues

spent prayerbooks hard handled—
worn with time—well-thumbed
men burdened once by sacks of flour—
laundry—lime—sit heavy haunched
hernia hung or hunched (as if)
s-bent before a needle or machine

in galleries above
decked in marriage wig and shawl
women whisper—offer shreds of melody
or odd amen—or nod with lolling head
onbreast onbelly onhip
in slow cascade of flesh
earthmother staid in spite of sprawl

(their sons this sabbath gone to weekday toil
underlay of ages washed away in seachange
 —cleft by quake of shifting soil)

at open windows—scattered—small
children lean out listening
for the great shofar of carhorns
or jericho shouts of stickball
in the street below

———

clean-press, jerk

dubin
indelicately
soiled
indubitably
all gaberdines
in care
with spilled
sardines
sardonically

and customers
would swear
he was
a dirty
sew and sew
for all repair

———

Italians

scattered one a block
differed by degrees of lard or lean
and latitudes of sacred or obscene

Joe Buffone

twice a day
would drink two quarts of beer
which Joey Jr. bore on credit
from the grocery store
and then careen through local streets
construction truck aswerve
sideswipe a car or two or jump a curb
and on a wilder spree
destroy a fence or raze a tree

at times he'd haul himself to Berger's store
where fly half-zipped but drink secure
he'd touch the grocer to the quick:
"hey, Berg', how big you dick?"

Milk-fed Dazzos

more respectably
comprised a living genealogy
their house a well-worn Mother Goose's shoe
that pinched as girths and generations grew

boldest of them all was young Marie
enfant terrible yet prodigy
who kept a pax romana with her fist
and told the boys their place but never kissed

others in rotund serenity
spilled from porch and window carelessly
soaking up an afternoon of sun
when dairy route deliveries were done
though one great uncle found some light employ
as Ezrath Akhim's faithful Shabbes goy

Pasta-less Pasquinis

                                        most austere

wore black all year
faces gaunt as if ahaunt
with sacred fear
seeming sworn to silence
hair close shorn
or worn pulled back severe

a mother with her mother
and two sons
the women paired like dour nuns
in glare and scowl
framed by swathing shawl
and close-drawn cowl

yet madonna-like withal
heart's-candle kindled
for the older boy
(their aspiration
not the least in doubt
for his vocation as a priest)
whose name prophetic
 augured well— Emmanuel

but oh that flaxen fiend of hell
the second son—no recluse
but wanton-passioned and profuse
battening on sweets
rioting in halls
raving through streets
scribbling schoolyard walls
a pagan of delight
taste touch sound sight
though down the dark Pasquini mind
a grim rebuke stood stark:
"Vincent, tempt us not—
lest your affront
should end at your behind!

———

autograph 7: kiss 1

in a doorway
her mouth on his
softdrawn

in slow implosion
walls give way
all breath all balance
gone

———

suicides

(for a. c. p.)

puppet on a string
he seemed to move
against his will
in scattered spasm—
footdrag headloll armflail—
all messages across
the neural chasm
lost, altered, shunted, failed

held to bare civility
by thinnest threads
he lived at home
long past maturity
and worked a meager job
beneath his means:
his public polity was self-defense—
thicktongue spittlelip slackjaw—
jesting at his own expense

until with deftness unsurmised
he fit the hempen twist
and left his last dependency
a stark surprise

(for –, sans garland of flowers)

distraught with study
a fiddlestring too taut

nerves ratcheted
for household nag and natter

fists clenched against himself
for appetites unsought

he found release
through ancient therapies

bath and blood let
—greatly overwrought—

and lay afloat
beneath a ruddy wash

beyond despair of is
inviolate of ought

———

enterprise

in their children's shop
sylvie and sol
childless

---

the-ater

Ambassador entrance
on wet sundays
 smelled of caramel
and damp carpet
enticing double feature
of a two-bit Diplomacy

---

lullaby

heartstrung horsehair thick
slow fiddle tunes adrift in august ooze
(cement at simmer as if ovenstones)
ripple summergelid afternoons

for housewives' hear
faith and flesh at ease
past giving of the law
dark eyes all aglaze
or belz a mythic blear
indolent in honeysplurge
before the days of awe

heavily dispursed sigh rent
wafted coin languoring
in afterair delay descent
till pocket drawn below
all gravity backbowed
songspent

a liltless lull—rechoired time
which childrenshriek dispels
a cry for harder currency
to clamoring of ice cream bells

---

jailbird jack

in his dissent
from parents' piety
he fell to petty theft
and spent his time
(impenitent)
on marvel comics
supplanting moses' tablets
with a double set
and freed from bondage
led no people
through a parted sea
but sped himself
(cain and ethan branded)
on racer wheels
through hardwood aisles
at a&p

———

autograph 8: transformation

sounding summons
unto far parlor corners
an orchestra this afternoon
turns tenement to hallowed hall

and she sun-mottled
with brindle-blinded light
suppliant ministrant and choir
moves marbled masqued
black leotard upon her white

at wordless prayer
all surge of flesh resolves
once whispered "cara"
purged and stilled
for holyfire awhorl
in carved carrara

———

barbershop

at sam's—a one-man union shop—
the scissors sang
but not as well as he
or soloists and orchestras
on 'qxr or 'nyc
(with sam himself at twin batons
of comb and shears)
or being shorn
a sweet-voiced child
with praises of "canary"
set to song

while at the rear
pinochle players
in cacophony
attacked each lay
or done—at last—at best
melded into hum

on a spare chair
randomly
a racing form and daily worker
paired in odd duet
a vaudeville or burlesque
of probability

———

borderlands 3

at van sinderen
the great wall halts
far eastern hordes
save those consigned above
who still hold sway
manhattan bound as one
almighty el strap hung
in a newlots line

or fused below
in wizardream
old alchemy
of asphalt into gold
transmuted tracts
of base democracy
while smokehouse whitefish
drip illusive gilt
upon less philo
sophic cobblestones
paving hellsway
with nitrosomines

———

witness

alone
in lengthened shadows of diminished day
the rabbi sinks in his seat of honor
shrivels, shrinks in a black suit,
bowed with downcast gaze

the sexton's deputy
who jesting as he strolled the aisles
once swore he knew a single blessing
—over schnapps—
amends all raucous stalking
silent now, mirthless
in his slow and dark patrol

one by one
the faithful enter
(with a distant nod)
and soon succumb (well-spaced)
to speechless solitude;
the skeptic sits beside his son
just come of age:
equally apart

we knew

(in that gathered hush and gloom)
scant years after Auschwitz
bare decades past the last blood libel
since the last pogrom

we knew

(it was our own shaved heads, slit trouser legs,
our own skins lashed with leather and the metal clamps)
confirmed in millennial memory

we knew

(charged with untold voltages of sabbath light)
that Friday afternoon they killed the Rosenbergs
that it could happen

AGAIN

———

autograph 9: triple play

in the mirror

whitecreme covers
dustdown smudge
as razored hand
raised in shear will sheer
hovers doubledged
above a fresh face
in a new year

behind

adept and master
of such bladed ways
he guides with deft touch
and words of praise

out of scene

she whispers
small sorrow
(neither sob nor keen)
— too soon too soon—
for such a severing

———

Buck Weinstein

Buck Weinstein charged a dollar at the office—
two at home. Better, though, at home,
making paper boats for little boys,
or rings for little girls with arrowed hearts
and two sets of initials—theirs and his.

Still, the waiting room would do—enough
chairs, magazines, a console radio.
His office too—with books in wooden cases
and a huge old desk. Though his exam-
ination room was bare—a table, chair,
some cabinets and drawers—but no machines:
xray, ekg, fluoroscope or diathermy.
Clinics were the place for three of these,
and as for heat, a water bottle was as good,
or mustard plasters in a stubborn case:
better that way, simpler for sure.
He lived above his office,
caring for a sister and his mother.
His heart was weak besides. It wouldn't stand
the stress of added electricity.

Once a year the high school kids showed up,
and he examined them before he signed
their notes. (Judy Jaffe, sensuous and seventeen,
swore he turned beet red and looked away
while listening to her chest.)

You went to him for colds, an ingrown toenail, or a sprain.
You called hm in to tell you what you knew yourself—
the spots are chicken-pox; the lumps are mumps.
With such a fee, and lack of frills, timidity,
No one called him if it looked like grippe,
or if a fever went beyond a hundred three.

He was, for instance, number ten or so
on Bubbe's list—hardly a professor.
But his degree from Glasgow, framed in black,
hung plainly on his office wall, and when
Fran broke her wrist, he diagnosed the fracture
perfectly. Too delicate to set himself,
he sent her to a specialist, and warned against
the Brownsville Butcher Shop—
he hated that hospital—Beth-El.

What he liked was music. He tuned his radio
to QXR, and sometimes set aside
his evening hours for going to the Met.
Returning home one frosty opera night,
He slogged apace through snow against the wind.
Then swifter still up front-door steps—and fell.
His sister found him lying there next morning.

The streets that day were noisy with the news.
And in the synagogues whispers over prayers
—*Veinshtin iz geshtorben*—were louder than usual.
Hundreds turned out for his funeral.

———

autograph 10: nocturne

parents deceived, they met to spend the night
wandering through nearly soundless streets
pondering —wondering— the "why" of us
till past moonset and a risen sun
and seated now upon their high school steps
knew the answer was what they had done

_____

delis

(i) artiste

deft at white & white
he daubed in gold—
furled, folded, rolled—
his finished forms
fanned end to end
in sunburst signature:
miró of mustard
picasso of paper cones

(ii) joe's

wistful at his window
beside the grill
he watches snowflakes
feint and fall
calling to mind
his wanwife
blood run thin
long ill and lately gone
leaving their smallchild
now seated (schoolday done)
hunched over homework
in bentwood chair
and him mid red red meats
standing silent and astare

(3) morph

in huddling hovels
crushed among tenements
corned beef and knishes
at wandwave of projects
turn to chicken and ribs

––––––––––

Recollection

When we stood—boys together—
At curb's edge,
Pissing in great arcs over the gutter,
At times beyond all dreams
And past desire,
Crossing each other's streams
And blending them to majesty of amber—
We did not see
The trickle ending on our shoes
But plash against a horseshit clod
Or patch of tar.
Even now, we can't remember.

Glossary and Notes

Entries are listed in order of appearance in the collection. Glossed words in languages other than English are predominantly those from Yiddish or Hebrew.

Reelpolitik
shpilst?. Do you play?

Freiheit. Freedom, the name of a Yiddish newspaper of far left bent.

territorial imperative
This game for two called "Land," akin to mumblety-peg, was played by throwing a pen knife so that it stuck in an opponent's territory (half a square drawn on the diagonal to begin with), scratching a line through the territory following the angle of the blade, and annexing one of the new pieces by erasing the appropriate portion of the original border. The object was to acquire as much new land as possible although rules for "winning" were various and local.

festival jazz
Ostrolenk. Ostrolenka, a city in northeastern Poland. Residents of particular places often formed their own congregations upon immigrating.

te-ki-ah sheh-vah-rim te-ru-ah. Hebrew for ritual series of notes sounded by the shofar (ram's horn) during services for Rosh Hashanah (New Year) and at the conclusion of Yom Kippur (Day of Atonement).

Russians

Hakenkreuz. A hooked cross, the Nazi symbol commonly and erroneously referred to as the swastika.

whet whether

tishri. The month of the Jewish calendar, corresponding to September/October, that introduces the New Year.

Menakhem Mendel

tokhes. Buttocks; backside.

The Ballad of Harry Heller

two sewers. The distance between one manhole cover and a third.

spaldeen. A hard, hollow pink ball made by the. Spalding company and used in various street games, particularly stickball, and, as here, punchball.

lunar litany

Following a lunar calendar, traditional Judaism marks the advent of each new month with special prayers, often recited outdoors at evening services.

Italians

Ezrath Akhim. A synagogue name roughly translated as "brothers helping brothers."

Shabbes goy. Gentile hired by Orthodox Jews to perform actions forbidden to them on the Sabbath, in this instance primarily the turning on and off of electric lights.

auntiquities

Kings Park. A section of Smithtown, Long Island housing a psychiatric hospital.

lullaby

dark eyes. A popular Russian song ("Ochi Chyornye").

Belz. A Ukrainian (at times, Polish) town that is the subject of the wistful Yiddish song "Mein Shtetele Belz" ("My Little Town of Belz").

barber shop

racing form. Then, as now, *The Daily Racing Form* published information each day about horses and races at various tracks.

daily worker. Ultimately an organ of the American Communist Party, *The Daily Worker* was published between 1924 and 1948.

Buck Weinstein

Bubbe's. Grandma's.

Veinshtin iz geshtorben. Weinstein has died.

Acknowledgments

The poems in *Brownsville* that have been published previously, some under other titles, are listed below. The list follows their order of appearance in the collection.

"Manifest Destiny." *The Hyper Texts* (Fall) 2006.
"borderlands (ii): the avenue/winter night" appeared as "The Avenue/Winter Night." *The HyperTexts* (Fall) 2006.
"auntiquities." *The HyperTexts* (Fall) 2006.

"autograph 6: childsplay" appeared as "Childsplay." *Poetry on the Parkway* (1976): n.p.

"autograph 8: transformation" appeared as "Transformation." *Salome*(Summer 1982): 20.

"witness" appeared as "Afterword" in Nelly Toll, *When Memory Speaks*. Westport: Praeger,1998: 82.

"suicides (i) (for a. c. p.)" appeared as "For S. B." in *Glassworks* (Fall 2011): 37.

Also by Martin Itzkowitz

The Days of Solomon Kahn

Spent Lives

The Days of Solomon Kahn

Written as an edited translation of an imagined journal kept in Yiddish, *The Days of Solomon Kahn* presents the experiences and world view of an immigrant from czarist Russia during the first half of the twentieth century. A mix of public and personal concerns, the entries are at times serious, at times humorous, at times both.

Spent Lives

Spent Lives is a collection of eleven stories set in the modern era that presents through its characters the varied life experiences of Jewish Americans in the second and third generations after the "great wave" of immigration from Eastern Europe.

www.ingramcontent.com/pod-product-compliance
Lightning Source LLC
Chambersburg PA
CBHW031244120626
46545CB00007B/2643